Stock Market Investing

A practical guide to approaching stock markets to make money and build passive income streams through easy, simple and long-term profitable strategies

Joshua Kratter

Table of contents

DISCLAIMER

The opinions and ideas of the author contained in this publication are designed to educate the reader in an informative and helpful manner. While we accept that the instructions will not suit every reader, it is only to be expected that the recipes might not gel with everyone. Use the book responsibly and at your own risk. This work with all its contents, does not guarantee correctness, completion, quality or correctness of the provided information. Always check with your medical practitioner should you be unsure whether to follow a low carb eating plan. Misinformation or misprints cannot be completely eliminated. Human error is real!

INTRODUCTION

Investing can be defined as the act of spending money or capital on endeavors with the expectation of receiving additional income or profit. Essentially, it is a completely different way to think about the way money is made. Growing up, many of us learnt that we can only earn income by working and this is exactly what many people are doing right now. However, there is one big issue and that is if you want more money, you're probably going to have to work for more hours. This probably won't make that much money for you and will exhaust you both mentally and physically. Also, you can't possibly create another version of yourself to increase the time you spend time working. Investing your money isn't going to maximize the potential of your earning whether you choose or not to work overtime, get a bonus, or look for another job.

There are various ways you can choose to make any investment. This involves placing money into stocks, mutual funds, real estate, and even investing in other businesses. Experts refer to these choices as investment vehicles, which each one having its benefits and drawbacks. However, you must choose an investment vehicle after you have spent enough time looking through the different options and understanding them. You should also avoid following others 'investment strategies because success in the investing world differs from one person to another. For example, someone might be more comfortable investing in three investment vehicles. They have been in the field for years whereas this isn't recommended for someone who is just starting because they are most likely going to get confused. It is always better to succeed in one and then jump to the next one.

One important thing you need to understand is that investment is completely different from gambling. Gambling involves you placing money at risk by bettering on new results with the hope that you will win money. At gambling the odds are always against you however in investment you can shift the odds to your advantage. However, some of the confusion between investing and gambling can come from the way people use investment vehicles. For example, purchasing a stock because someone told you is just like placing bets in casinos. However, real investors don't simply throw their money at any investment out there; they perform analysis and spend capital and money only where reasonable profits are expected. Even though there is a risk, there aren't any guarantees whatsoever and investing is more than just hoping that you get lucky.

This book includes a detailed explanation on investing, its various associated terminologies, methods of investing, among other important information that will get you started in the world of investing.

CHAPTER 1 - BASICS ON INVESTING

EXPLORING POSSIBILITIES OF INVESTING

The world of investing is diverse and full of different possibilities and chances. One of the best things about the investment world is that there is a place for everyone. Whether you're a beginner or have been investing for years, have long or short-term goals, or simply just want to experiment a bit, you will find something suitable for you. However, it is essential to understand that this isn't a get rich quick scheme where you're going to make millions overnight. You will first need to educate yourself about its different aspects, set your goals, and choose what you want to invest in. Becoming successful in the investment world requires hard work, dedication, and a proper understanding of its different aspects. This chapter is going to involve a detailed explanation of the different types of investment vehicles, their benefits and drawbacks, and the steps required to successfully invest in them successfully.

STOCKS & BONDS

Stocks and bonds are two important investing building blocks. Stocks are direct ownerships in businesses whereas bonds are loans. Various products related to stock and bonds have been created during the past few years, such as mutual funds and default swaps. These investment choices are great, but with these choices is the responsibility to recognize which of these choices help you in fulfilling financial goals. Buying stock means that you're going to take ownership in a specific entity. One of the main advantages of direct ownership is that the process is fairly easily and there aren't any associated management fees or other individuals involved. The price of buying individual stocks is affordable – many times, it can cost $10 or even less. However, one of the drawbacks is that you have to stay updated on how the investments are doing all the time. This is why you need to have a proper understanding of accounting principles at least and stay updated with company reports. Buying bonds means that you're going to loan money to entities, like businesses, people, or governments. Purchasing a bond is exactly like purchasing a car: you need to negotiate so you can get the better price. Owning a bond needs you to know the claims you have to the entity's assets if bankruptcy takes place.

Changes in the market can have a big impact on stock markets as well.

The Dow jones is considered to be one of the biggest financial markets. Every day, traders engage in $5 trillion worth of exchange transactions. Due to Dow Jones being an international marketplace, events taking place from all over the world can have an instant impact on currency values and rates of exchange. This report is going to explain the impact of global events on the Dow Jones market (Jones & Khanna, 2006). During the year 2015, several events affected Dow Jones such as the Greek crisis, the decrease of oil prices, and the change that took place in the Federal Reserve interest rate policies,

Greek crisis and its impact on Dow Jones

When the Greek crisis took place, Dow Jones decreased to the lowest rates and it was considered to be the worst day for it in 2015. The significant decline was a result of Greece closing their banking system, central bank executing controls to stop money from leaving Greece, and all the different protests that took place as a result where citizens weren't happy with all the changes that were taking place (Consolandi, 2009).

Traders stated that the selling process was mainly broad based. Volumes of trading were somewhat high, with 7.3 billion shares continuously changing hands when compared with the annual data average of about 6 billion shares. The Dow industrials decreased by 350.33 points, to 17596.35. On the other hand, the S&P 500 decreased by 43.85 points to 2057.64. Finally, the Nasdaq index decreased by 122.04 to 4958.47.

Decrease of oil prices

In August, oil prices decreased below $40 per barrel and this is the first time this happens since 2009 amongst increased agreement that cheap crude is going to stay. Oil investors, who figured it out early that prices are going to recover during the second half of this year, now state that rebounds are most likely going to happen before 2017. Government forecasters decreased their estimates of oil prices to $60 per barrel during 2016.

The change in opinions is mainly because of oil producers in the United States, who are continuously pumping crude at record levels. An unexpected rally of prices that took place in some companies enabled companies to lock profitable prices for 2016. Brent crude, the international benchmark decreased by 2.5% to about $45.46 per barrel.

Federal Reserve interest rate policies

During the end of 2015, the Federal Reserve decided to increase interest rates, and this had a significant impact on the stock market, especially Dow Jones. This is the first time this happens in nine years and no one excepted this surge to take place. This had a positive impact on stocks, where the Down Jones increased by 185 points, Nasdaq increased by 1.1%, and the S&P 500 increased by 1.3%. It was a unanimous decision to increase rates and Fed officially asserted that even though the rates increase, the policy will still be accommodative. The Federal Reserve policy has helped in increasing stocks in the United States since the crisis took place. The dollar decreased against the euro. Also, the yen government bonds became stronger, pushing yields to an even lower rate. Stocks that pay out dividends high in value, which has continuously rallied in previous years among low rates of interest, resulted in the S$P 500 become higher after the decision of the Feds. The prices of crude oil increased to 4.9 per barrel, snapping rebounds for two days, after an increase in the crude supplies in the United States. This surge took place suddenly and wasn't expected at all. On the other hand, stock markets in other regions such as Europe and Asia weren't open in trading when the Federal Reserve released their new decision. This is one of the very few events that had a positive impact on Dow Jones and associated trading processes during 2015.

During the year 2015, several events affected Dow Jones such as the Greek crisis, the decrease of oil prices, and the change that took place in the Federal Reserve interest rate policies. This report included an explanation of the different events that impact Dow Jones. These situations include wars, natural disasters, and political events. Each of these events has both a negative and positive impact and it can be difficult to determine what exactly is going to take place and whether traders are going to gain or lose money. Even though traders can predict certain events before they take place, it is difficult to do this in every situation, especially like the case of natural disasters where no one knows when they're going to take place. Also, it is difficult to predict how an event is going to impact Dow Jones. As demonstrated in this research, there are some cases where wars in example impacted S & P positively and some cases where it affected it negatively.

MUTUAL FUNDS

Mutual funds are a method for investors to place their money in one place, so they can increase purchasing power and decrease execution costs. One of the drawbacks to mutual funds is the different associated fees. All types of mutual funds charge a fee, and many even charge sales fees on top of management fees. If you choose to invest in mutual funds, make sure you completely understand the fees you have to pay and the investment fund mandates. It is essential to note that you will only be able to trade mutual funds once per day and that is when the markets close.

EXCHANGE TRADED FUND

The Exchange Traded Fund (ETF) is a financial innovation that is newer than the other investment vehicles. The ETF places mutual funds into an investment vehicle that trades likes stocks and works due to the one price law. The one price law explains that when two investments track the same thing, then the profit and return from holding these investments is going to be the same as well. For example, when investments are overvalued, you are going to sell these overvalued investments and then use the returns to purchase more of the accurately priced investments. However, if you decide to buy an ETF, make sure you pay attention to what the investments being tracked are, and the amount of ETF shares being purchased and sold daily.

It is essential to check on who is responsible for sponsoring ETF functions and make sure that it is done properly. All these different investment vehicles are excellent investment tools and every one of them has a place in a well-diversified plan.

REAL ESTATE

Investing in real estate has become more popular during the last fifty years and is considered to be one of the most important investment vehicles. Even though the real estate market has numerous opportunities for making money, purchasing, and owning real estate, this is more complicated than simply investing in stocks or bonds.

Basic rental properties

This is one of the oldest real estate investment practices. It involves someone purchasing property and then renting it to tenants. Owners are responsible for paying mortgages and costs associated with maintaining the property. Landlords can charge extra to cover costs mentioned above and to produce a profit for themselves. Furthermore, the property can be appreciated in terms of value.

A main difference between rental properties and other investment types is the time and work spent on maintaining the investment. When you purchase a stock, it's going to stay in your investing accounting and increase in value.

Real estate investment groups

Real estate investment groups are similar to mutual funds for rental properties and are the perfect choice for you if you aren't looking for the hassle of taking responsibility as landlords. An example of this would be purchasing apartment blocks and then enabling investors to purchase them through the company, therefore joining investment groups. Single investors can own numerous or one complex. In exchange for this type of management, the company is going to be able to take a part of the monthly rent. Even though this is safe way to enter the real estate investment sector, many groups are susceptible to the exact fees that trouble the mutual fund sector.

REAL ESTATE TRADING

This is considered to be real estate's wild side. Real estate traders purchase properties to hold them for a specific amount of time, often not more than four months, hoping to sell them in return for a profit. This technique is known as flipping properties as well and depends on purchasing properties that are undervalued or in hot markets. Pure property filters aren't just going to put money in real estate for enhancement's where the investment needs to have intrinsic values so that it can gain profit without any alteration or they won't even consider it. Flipping in this way is considered to be a short-term investment. If property fillers become caught in situations where they can't unload properties, this can be overwhelming, as these investors don't maintain enough cash so that they can pay mortgages on long term properties. This can result in continued losses for real estate traders who are not able to offload real estate in poor performing markets.

REITS

An interesting fact is that real estate has been in the world since our ancestors, so it isn't surprising that Wall Street was successful in finding a way to transform real estate into an instrument that is publicly traded. Real estate investment trusts (REIT) is created when an organization (or the trust) utilizes the money of investors to operate and buy income properties. REITs are purchased and sold on major types of exchanges, like other types of stocks. Companies have to pay 90% of their taxable profits in the type of dividends, to maintain its position as an REIT.

RUNNING SMALL BUSINESS AND INVESTING IN THEM

Investing in other start-ups

Investing in established businesses or start-ups can be a successful investment and more profitable than you expect. Venture capital funds that are publicly traded usually invest in different start-ups, resulting in then creating a diverse portfolio of companies that have the potential to be successful. With only one investment, you are going to be able to access a diverse portfolio of companies that have successfully passed venture capital tests. There are usually many chances to make direct investments in start-ups that you have some knowledge or experience in, where you can exchange equity stakes for the funding you provide.

Both investment types have a level of outsized risks that matches outsized rewards if the business proves to be successful. Therefore, it is essential to do research and invest in these opportunities. Investing your money through venture capital is the most popular alternative. You don't necessarily have to leave your job or establish an office; you will only have to purchase shares.

Partner Up

Instead of only investing in businesses for equity stakes, you should consider taking it into another level and become a partner in a business that already exists. This is going to include making daily work in the organization, focusing on things founders don't necessarily have enough time for, such as market or accounting, or it can be a larger role. Not only is it going to provide you with the entrepreneurship experience, but enable you to select the types of tasks and work you would like to do.

ENTREPRENEURSHIP

Another choice is becoming an entrepreneurship in larger companies. Many organizations have established structures that persuade employees to lead new organizational lines in exchange for equity and bonuses. When you find an organization that has a strong innovation culture, you are going to be able to build your organization within it, with the benefit of having start-up capital from the start and personal risk is going to decrease as well.

You could even be able to begin an entrepreneurship program at your work by asking for an amount of your time to work on projects that have bonus structures. To boost your argument, you can always boost to companies such as 3M and Intel, two companies which experienced significant growth throughout a period when entrepreneurship defined corporate culture.

PURCHASE A FRANCHISE

Businesses in boxes are one way to steer away from the hassles involved with beginning from scratch. Owners of franchises already follow scripts that have already proven to be successful. The advantages of franchises include dealing with a well-known brand, having resources to go back to, and economies of scale created by franchises.

The main disadvantage is the cost of purchasing a franchise and its associated royalties, which are steep most of the time. Individuals looking for the true entrepreneur experience are going to have issues with various limitations added by franchise offices. However, franchises usually have a powerful support network and are known for having high rates of success.

Chapter 2 – Classifying Stocks

There is a lot more involved in investing in the stock market than simply purchasing shares, or stock, in a company and calling it a day. There are several different classes of stocks, all of which can be classified into two types: Common Stock and Preferred Stock. In this chapter, I am going to discuss the different stock classes that fall into these two categories, and what it means to buy the different stock types.

Common Stock

As the name suggests, common stock is, simply put, common. This is the type of stock that most people are talking about when discussing stocks in general, and the majority of stock on the stock market is issued in the form of common stock. In essence, common shares represent ownership in a company, and a claim, or dividends, in a portion of its profits.

Investors are allowed one vote per share to elect members of the board, who will then oversee the major decisions that the management makes. When considering the long term, common stock yields much higher returns than pretty much all other investments, using capital growth. This higher return does, however, come at a cost, as the majority of common stocks come with the highest risk attached.

If a company goes bankrupt and is forced to liquidate, those who hold common shares will not receive any cash until the bondholders, creditors, and preferred shareholders are paid - hence the risk. This leads us to the second type of stock: preferred stock.

PREFERRED STOCK

Like common stock, preferred stock is a representation of some degree of ownership of a company. However, unlike common stock, it does not come with the same rights for voting, though this may vary from company to company. Investors are generally guaranteed a fixed dividend forever with preferred shares. This differs from common stock in that common stock does not have any guaranteed dividends.

Another advantage to preferred stock is that, in the event of liquidation, shareholders with preferred stock are paid before those with common stocks, albeit still after debt holders. Preferred stock can also be callable, which means that the company can purchase the shares from its shareholders at a time of their choosing, for any reason, usually for a premium as well.

Many people consider preferred stock to be more of a debt than an equity. It helps to think of these shares as being in the place between common shares and bonds.

OTHER STOCK TYPES

Industry

Companies are generally divided by industry, which are usually called sectors. Stocks that belong to the same sector, such as energy or technology sectors, might shift together in response to economic or market events. This is why it is so important to diversify your portfolio by investing in stocks across various sectors.

Company size

If you've done any research about the stock market, you may have heard the terms mid-cap or large-cap.

These terms refer to the capitalization of the market, or how valuable a company is. Usually, companies are separated into three 'buckets' by size:

- Large cap: **market value of $10 billion or more**

- Mid cap: **market value between $2 billion and $10 billion**

- Small cap: **market value between $300 million and $2 billion**

Style

Sometimes, stocks are described as value or growth. Growth stocks are provided by companies that are either growing at a rapid pace, or are expected to grow quickly. Investors are usually willing to pay more for these kinds of stocks since they can expect greater returns.

On the other hand, value stocks are basically on sale. These are the stocks that have been deemed undervalued and underpriced by investors. It is assumed that these stocks are going to appreciate, as they are either suffering from a short-term event or going undetected.

Location

Stocks are also usually grouped by their geographical location. You can diversify your investment portfolio by investing in companies that do business internationally, as well as in emerging markets, which are market areas that are expected to experience some growth.

Now that we've covered the basic categories of stock, it's time to look at their various classifications and the implications that these classifications have.

CLASS OF SHARES/STOCKS

To understand the different classes of stocks, it's important to understand what a class of shares is.

What is a class of share?

Essentially, a class of shares is a type of stock listed by a company that is differentiated by the level of voting rights received by the shareholders. For example, a company could have two classes of shares, or classes of stock, which we'll call Class A and Class B for the sake of simplicity. Company owners that have owned their company privately and choose to go public usually create Class A and Class B stock structures with different rights for voting.

This is done so that they can maintain control, and well as ensure that the company is not so easily targeted for a takeover. One of the most common of the stock classes is advisory shares, which are also called advisor shares. This stock type is given to business advisors in exchange for their expertise and insight.

The advisors that this type of stock option is offered to are founders of companies, or high-level executives. Usually, advisor shares invest monthly over about two years, one a no-cliff schedule, and 100% trigger acceleration.

Understanding these classes

The term 'class of shares' can also refer to the various share classes that exist for numerous mutual funds. There are three different share classes: Class A, Class B, and Class C. These classes hold different sales charges, operating expenses, and 12b-1 fees. Whether referring to the multiple share classes that advisor-sold mutual funds offer, or the different classes of a company's stock, both of these cases refer to the different costs and rights owned by those who hold each share class. Simple, right?

Mutual fund share classes

Mutual funds sold by advisors can have different classes, each class having a fee structure and a unique sales charge. Class A mutual fund shares have lower 12b-1 fees, charge a front-end load and have operating expenses that are below average. Class B mutual fund shares have higher 12b-1 fees, charge a back-end load, and have higher operating expenses. Finally, Class C mutual fund shares do not have a front-end load, though back-end loads still apply, are considered level-load and have higher-than-average operating expenses.

Contingent deferred sales charge (CDSC), or the back-end load, can be eliminated or reduced, depending on the duration for which shares have been held. Class B shares will usually have a CDSC that is gone in as little as one year from the date they were purchased. Class C shares will generally start with a high CDSC, which will only completely disappear after about 5-10 years.

CHAPTER 3 - RISK AND RETURN

Understanding the concept of risk, returns, diversification, and portfolio building is extremely important in the investment world. This chapter includes a detailed explanation of these aspects along with steps on how to build a diversification portfolio successfully.

RISK AND RETURNS IN THE INVESTMENT WORLD

There are risks that investors face in the investment world. Many of these risks are serious, and if not addressed properly, can have negative long-term impacts on the ability to fulfill your financial goals, and others are simply considered to be driven by feelings and human bias. A type of risk includes the organization you're investing in going bankrupt, which means that you're going to lose money. However, this doesn't necessarily happen a lot and the results can be decreased by diversification and not following the promise of high returns.

Diversification is an effective way to manage risk. Usually, investment advisers and managers speak about risks like interest rate, market, and currency risks. Every one of them can result in returns and profits being less than what is expected and, in many times, even negative. However, they are all considered to be manageable and are essential parts of the more significant risks.

This usually takes place when investors are too conservative, inexperienced, greedy, or simply give up a lot of their returns for taxes or fees. In many cases, there are going to be event risks that are going to have an unpredicted negative effect on your assets values. As example of this would be foot disease in New Zealand.

However, the good news is that there are principles you can follow to manage risk such as: successfully

- There are no returns without associated risks. The returns are only half of the equation. Earnings that are higher than long-term profits usually have more short-term risks. The profits and rewards are reaped by investors who manage these risks and don't search to prevent risk altogether. Risk is considered to be the other side of the chance of the investment. What is essential is that risks you take are appropriate for the investment you're making and the time frame of your financial goals.
- Risks should be properly understood and returns have to be completely transparent. When risks associated with investments aren't understood properly, it is going to be difficult to manage them. If returns 'sources aren't transparent, associated risks are a lot higher as of the unknown. Investing first needs information and understanding and using common sense.
- Experience and count of judgement. Risks can't be controlled only using mathematical models or ratios. A risk reward tool is used by many investors to conduct a comparison of an investment's expected returns to the risk amount undertaken to get these returns. They are simply a tool that creates the basis of the right judgment.

- Diversification. This is going to be explained in more detail in the next part. Diversification includes various investments, in one asset class, decreases risk without changing expected returns. Diversification also decreases uncertainty level that the outcome of returns is usually different.
- Consistency. A rigorous and steady approach will lead in managing risk better than a process that is constantly changing. It also offers an improved framework for comprehending the outcome. It is also essential to comprehend where competitive advantages can be found and the decisions that can be made based on this guess.

CONCEPT OF PORTFOLIO BUILDING AND DIVERSIFICATION

There are some situations where checking the value of your investments can be tempting. However, this is just when feelings have a strange way of stopping the minds of even the most experienced investors. This is the main reason why you have to check your portfolio regularly, at least the investment mix once per day or any time you notice your financial condition changing significantly. For example, when you lose your job or receive a significant bonus. Setting your strategic asset share are among the most significant ingredient in your long-term success.

WHY DIVERSIFYING

The main goal of diversification isn't only to enhance performance as it won't guarantee profits or losses. However, once you select to focus on a risk level depending on your objectives time horizon, and acceptance for volatility, diversification can offer the chance to enhance returns for that risk level. To successfully create a diversified portfolio, you need to search for assets and investment vehicles, whose returns didn't move in the same direction. This way, when a part of your portfolio isn't performing well, the remaining part of your portfolio will be growing. Therefore, you will be able to offset the effect on poor performance and prevent it from negatively impacting your portfolio. Another essential aspect of creating a well-diversified portfolio is that you can attempt to stay diversified within every investment type. With the holdings of your stocks, make sure you avoid single stock overconcentration. For example, there is the possibility that you don't want a stock to be worth more than 5% of your overall stock portfolio.

Diversification has proven to be successful

Throughout the 2008 bear market, various investment types have lost their value to an extent. Even though it seemed like diversification failed, it didn't. The significant asset classes were more correlated, and diversification still assisted buy-and-hold portfolio losses. Take into considered 3 hypothetical portfolios: a portfolio including 70% stocks, 25% short term investments and finally 25% bonds.

Diversification assisted reduce losses and maintain gains throughout the financial crisis

The asset's hypothetical value maintained untaxed accounts worth $100,000 in cash portfolios. This is a diversified portfolio including 49% local U.S. stocks, and 21% global stocks. By the end of February 2009, both stocks and diversified portfolio declined. However, they all lost half of their initial value. On the other hand, the diversified portfolio lost more than a third. Even though the diversified portfolio could have decreased, diversification would have assisted in decreasing losses when compared with all-stock portfolios.

Watching stocks and diversified portfolio decrease if the type of situation that can stress investors or stir their emotions. This can sometimes result in making short-term and fast decisions, such as dumping stock holdings. Yes, keeping money in the form of cash could have sounded like a great idea during February 2009. However, look at what ended up happening when the market began becoming stable again.

5 years after being in the bottom, our created all-stock portfolio would have increased by 162.3% and the diversification portfolio would have been worth around 99.7% more. All stock portfolios experience the biggest improvement during the upswing of the markets. This is an excellent example of the way portfolios can gain less than all-stock portfolios and a lot more than portfolios that are all-cash. Now let's look at what ended up happening over a longer sequence. From January 2008

to February 2014, diversified portfolios increased by 29.9% whereas all-stock portfolios increased by 31.8%. This is mainly what diversification is all about where it doesn't necessarily increase profits in rising markets, but captures many of the gain while being less volatile than investing in various stocks

THE HIGH COST OF CHOOSING BAD TIMING

Why is it essential to have a level of risk you can live with? As the above chart demonstrates, diversified portfolios end up playing over time. However, the fact is that many investors face issues to realize the advantages of their investment tactics, individuals usually go after performance and buy higher-risk investments.

When the market faces issues, investors usually go for lower risk investment choices. These choices can result in missed chances during consequent market recoveries. The extent of underperformance by these investors has proven to be the worst in bear markets. Research have consistently demonstrated that returns gained by average stocks and bonds, fund investors lag usually by large margins, reported returns and profits of average stocks.

Research conducted from DALBAR demonstrates that fund investors follow markets in a significant manner.

This means that most of the decisions they make related to diversification generate lower returns than overall markets. Having a well thought plan that consists of suitable investment mixes and proper rebalancing can assist investors in overcoming these issues.

HOW TO BUILD A DIVERSIFIED PORTFOLIO

To begin, you are going to have to make sure that your investment vehicles and mix are aligned with your investment duration, financial requirements, and comfort with levels of volatility. Previous performance isn't a guarantee of how your investment vehicles will act or future results. Returns consist of reinvesting dividends and other types of earnings. However, it is essential to understand that diversification isn't a one-time task and investments usually change over time. The chart below demonstrates the difference between the performance of diversification portfolios in 1995 and 2015.

So, what takes place when you don't balance your portfolio? Let's examine an example portfolio over twenty years to show how changing markets, like the S&P 500's increase which took place in last years, can have an effect on investment mixes and risk levels in portfolios. Let's say the portfolio experienced a growth worth 80% in stocks, 10% in bonds, and 10% in short term investments during April 1995. Twenty years later, at the end of April 2015, this mix has completely changed, and all its components experienced an increase.

An important thing to understand is that previous performance doesn't necessarily guarantee profitable results, especially that stocks have had higher cost swings than money or bonds. In other words, when portfolios tilt towards stocks, they have the chance for bigger increases. The risk level of the portfolio was about 10% more than target mixes because of changes in the allocation of assets related with relative returns to the different investment vehicles. The yearly standard deviation of returns assesses the levels of risk associated with the portfolio gained every month, which demonstrated the variability of returns.

Let's now examine these levels of risk over time by taking two scenarios as an example. If investment mixes are rebalanced back to targets yearly, and if no revaluations took place (a purchase and hold technique). The levels of risk associated with purchase and hold portfolios differs widely than the ones of rebalanced portfolios. Throughout the time frame, this portfolio will have higher risks (yearly portfolio volatility). Rebalancing and reassessing your portfolio aren't only an exercise to decrease risk. The main goal here is to rearrange your investment mix so it is brought back to the expected levels of risk. Sometimes, this can mean decreasing risk levels by increasing portfolio portions in more conservative choices. However, this can mean increasing the risk so that you can get back to the target mix again. This involves increasing the amount of investments in asset classes that are more risky like stocks. You will have to create a strategy, select suitable investment, and carry out regular checkups to make sure that your portfolio is always on track. Below are three steps that are going to help you in achieving this:

I)KNOW WHAT YOU INVESTMENT MIX IS.

If you haven't done this already, select a combination of investment vehicles that you consider suitable for your investing objectives and goals. You should also take into consideration your finance, levels of volatility, and you will require the money you're investing. The more time you have to investment, the higher the appropriate level of investment vehicles in a portfolio. For example, stocks have always higher growth possibilities, and longer time frames can assist in decreasing volatility levels. Also, when you require the money in a couple of years, or if the idea of losing money is making you nervous, you should take into consideration allocating more to investments that are less volatile like bonds and short duration investments. When you do this, you are going to be trading the possibility of more returns for less levels of volatility.

II) EXAMINE YOUR PORTFOLIO REGULARLY

It is suggested that, whether you do this alone or using the help of investment professionals, you should monitor investment mixes yearly, or whenever the market conditions or financial circumstances end up changing. You must reassess your portfolio to fix any significant change that is going to impact your portfolio. A good idea is to considered rebalancing your portfolio is the stock allocation shifts away from the target by 10% points

III) REBALANCING YOUR PORTFOLIO

There are different ways to rebalance your investment portfolio. One of them is to sell these assets classes that you have a lot of and then reinvest these gains in those that are less than your target. However, selling securities in taxable accounts has different tax consequences. Therefore, you have to be sure to consider taxes when you're deciding to purchase or sell. Another way to do this is by rebalancing the portfolio without instant tax results in by investing the money have gradually or at the same time.

No matter what approach you decide to follow, one significant part of rebalancing is to do it in a manner that keeps your investing portfolio diversified in any investment type. Fulfilling your long-term goals needs balancing rewards and associated risks. Select the right investment mixes and then monitoring these choices can make a huge difference in your results.

CHAPTER 4 - GETTING STARTED

After choosing an investment vehicle and the type of portfolio you're interested in, the next step would be selecting an appropriate strategy. This chapter is going to include a detailed explanation of the investment process, how to set up goals successfully, and effective ways to create a portfolio.

FOLLOW THE INVESTMENT PROCESS

The investment process is divided into seven different steps, with each one being more important than the other.

- Purpose: You need to ensure that you have a proper understanding of the aim of your investments, concerning your goals and the reasons you're investing your money in them. You should have different short-term goals in the framework on a long-term plan. However, various investments are more suitable for various goals and this is why you have to take into consideration every goal separately and differently, and then search for synergies between these goals.
- Return: Choose the returns you need, in terms of immediate or long-term income. This also includes growth and development to achieve goals successfully. Income and components of growth are going to make up for the total profits and returns.
- Time frame: Choose the time frame you're investing for, so you can achieve and make

progress when it comes to achieving your objectives and goals. Your time frame is going to be a mixture of the timeframe you want to spend your money on (example: retirement) and the maximum amount of time you can wait before you see profits and any results. This is going to make you confident that you're on the right way to achieve your objectives and goals.

- Risk: choose which risks and the number of risks you're going to take. You should also choose risks and possible adverse results that can and have to be managed.
- Investment tactic: choose the investment strategy that is best for you in terms of balancing the requirements of your returns over the duration you're investing in.
- Assets: choose the type of assets (products) you are going to purchase to apply your plan.
- Review: Make sure you repeat these stages, as needed, based on any changes that take place to your objectives or any sudden circumstances that take place.

When you follow the seven-step investment strategy, you will find that you need assistance and recommendations if you're just starting out. If you don't need help, then that is great, and you can continue implementing the steps on your own. If you do, it is a great idea to discuss your objectives and goals with someone who is more professional and will help you in being objective. Likewise, when you identify assets for your investment strategy, you could need someone with a specific expertise. However, it is essential to remember that the more fees you pay to gain advice and help, the less returns you are probably going to end up with. The recommendations obtained should focus on enhancing the chance that you can fulfill your financial goals.

CREATE AN OVERVIEW OF YOU FINANCIALS AND DECIDE HOW MUCH YOU ARE WILLING TO USE FOR INVESTMENT AND THE IMPORTANCE OF MAINTAINING LIQUIDITY.

Creating an overview of the amount of money you're going to spend and understanding the concept of liquidity is important. Do you understand how easily accessible money is in the shape of cash and equivalent's? This is a liquidity assessment.

As you can see, this has a significant role in the financial lives and those of the stocks you purchase and sell. Beginning from a definition of it with examples of various types, we then going to examine how investment vehicles have an essential role in maintaining liquidity. It is essential to understand liquidity from other investors, especially when it comes to the stock market. Keep in mind that financial ratios could be used to assess the liquidity of an investment vehicle or a company.

Liquidity refers to how easy it is to transform assets to money (cash). Cash is considered to be the most liquid assets, and this is why it is always used for comparisons. On the other hand, deposit certificates are considered to be less liquid, as there is a penalty for changing them to cash right before their date of maturity. Also, savings bonds are considered to be quite liquid, because they're quickly sold at banks. Finally, the different shares of bonds, commodities, and stocks are considered to be somewhat liquid, as they are sold readily, and cash can be received in a couple of days. Any of these can be considered to be cash or equivalents of cash as they are converted to cash without any effort, even though this can sometimes be accompanied with a small penalty.

Moving down, we are going to run into different assets that require more effort and time before they could be considered to be cash. An example of this would be restricted shares, which has covenants dictating the way it can be sold. Other examples include items such as coins, arts, and other types of collectibles. If you are going to sell other collectors, you should receive full value, but this can take some time, even with the internet making it easier to some extent. If you decide to use a dealer, you are going to be able to receive quicker, but it is probably going to be less. The least type of liquid asset is real estate as it usually takes weeks, if not months to be successfully sold. When investing in assets, it is essential to take levels of liquidity in considered as it can be hard, or it can take a lot of time to chance certain types of assets into cash again.

Apart from selling assets, cash could be gained by borrowing against it. Even though this can be done privately between two individuals, it is usually done thought financial institutions. A financial institution has a lot more cash from depositors put together and can effectively fulfil the requirements of any borrower. Also, when depositors require cash instantly, this person isn't just going to withdraw it from the financial institution instead of going to borrowers and asking for payments of the whole note. Therefore, financial institutions act as intermediaries between the lenders and borrowers, resulting in a smooth money flow and fulfilling the requirements of every part of a loan.

LIQUIDITY AND STOCK MARKETS

When it comes to the stock market, liquidity has a different meaning, even though still connected how easily the assets, or stock shares, can be effectively changed to cash. The stock market is considered to be liquid if shares are rapidly sold and selling acts have little effect on the price of stocks. Usually, this translates to where shares are bought and traded and the amount of interest that the investors have in it. The stocks of companies traded on significant exchanges are considered to be liquid. Usually, 1% of the overall float trades daily, showing high interest degrees in stocks. Also, stocks of companies traded on pink sheets and over the counter are considered to be non-liquid, with a few, if not zero shares traded daily.

Another way to successfully judge company's stock liquidity is by examining bid/ask spread. When it comes to liquid spreads, like Microsoft and General Electric, spreads are considered to be a couple of pennies only, probably less than one percent of the overall price. However, when it comes to illiquid stocks, the spreads are considered to be a lot larger, resulting in a few percent of the overall price.

An important thing to take into consideration as an investor when putting an order, is the stock's liquidity. During ordinary market hours on significant exchanges, putting a limit order will lead to you getting the price of what you're looking for. This is especially true for non-liquid companies, or throughout after hours trading where fewer traders are going to be active. It is the most suitable to put a limited order as lower liquidities can result to a cost they wouldn't be willing to pay.

DEFINE FINANCIAL GOALS AND CREATE OVERVIEW OF EXPENSES (FINANCIAL TRIANGLE ⬜ LIQUIDITY, RETURN, SECURITY (MONEY).

The next and perhaps one of the most important steps is clearly defining short term and long-term goals. It is essential also to understand and follow the financial triangle, which includes liquidity, return, and security where they are all connected.

People invest for different reasons and this is why you must determine your financial goals, both long and short term. You could have to spend years on some goals whereas other can be achievable within a couple of days. Relatedly, it requires careful planning and a more balanced approach to fulfill long term goals while financing current ones successfully.

When you're creating the financial strategy, the main thing you have to do is figure out your short- and long-term goals. This will provide you with assurance of a promising financial future. With goals and an investment plan being identified, there will be a tendency to place your money in the wrong place with useless spending resulting in the possibility of financial trouble. Think of the goals you set as the framework for your investment plan. Every financial goal needs to have a time frame and is considered to be a milestone for future goals. Short term goals are different from long ones in timing. They are usually smaller in their scope and monetary amount with a specific target date for achieving them.

Example of short-term goals could involve buying household furniture, home improvements, or simply saving to invest in a stock. A short-term goal is one that you could want to achieve a couple of weeks to two years from the time you invest. Many investment experts explain that short term goals should involve eliminating any debt and having an overview of expenses.

IDENTIFY AND PRIORITIZE GOALS

The first thing you have to do is figure out the things you want in life. This could differ from purchasing a house to beginning a business or simply retiring based on your schedule. Without any goals, the returns you earn can be spent on things you don't necessarily require at that moment. Other than identifying financial goals, try to estimate the amount of expenses and money you are going to require so you can reach every goal. Creating a time frame for every short-term goal is important as well, especially when it comes to determining how many years it is going to take you to achieve this goal successfully.

Assessing finances and eliminating debt

Examine your current financial situation, such as credit card debt, loans, or mortgages. Before you begin investing money and spending money to achieve goals, you must eliminate any debt you have, especially ones that have high interest rates such as credit cards. This has to be your main short-term goal. Also, if you have purchased stocks and funds previously and these investments are doing well, make sure they fit into your plan. Understand what exactly you're basing the goals on. For example, if you're setting goals for retirement, you need to figure out the amount of years left until you retire, and the income amount you are going to need. The next short-term goal is enhancing savings by reducing on unnecessary spending. When you take a look at some of things you spend money on, you will notice that there are a lot of things you spend on that aren't necessary and you can use them in the investment process.

Asking for help in setting up a financial plan is a great idea as well if you're facing issues understanding certain aspects. Investment advisors who are experienced aren't only going to assist in identifying goals and evaluating a financial situation, but they are also going to choose investments that are matched with your objectives and goals. Also, investment advisors are specially trained, so they can find investments that are suitable with your strategy, risk place, and also taking into consideration different aspects of your life into consideration when creating an investment plan for you. Expert investment advisors also conduct regular follow-ups by continuously monitoring investments and ensure adjustments are made when required.

LONG-TERM GOALS

There are short term, long term, and goals that are simply in between. The difference between these categories is usually connected to the time it requires to fulfill the goals and the monetary commitment to fulfill them. Long term goals usually require years to be calculated. The most important long-term goal for everybody is saving for their retirement or making enough money so they can support the lifestyle they want on a long-term scale. One of the main steps involves excellent savings and creating a detailed financial plan when you are starting. This will enable you to stay on track throughout the process.

MONITOR INVESTMENTS REGULARLY

It is essential to check investment regularly. It is recommended to personally go through your portfolio every four months and meet with your advisor regularly. You should also manage risks by ensuring your selected assets allocations are still matching with your overall objectives and goals. Make suitable adjustments to investments only when required. The main benefit of having investment advisors is that they're going to be able to monitor funds and encourage various investments when needed. If something comes up when you're reviewing your plan, you can always revise it accordingly because this is going to help you in identifying new goals as well.

DEFINE A PORTFOLIO OF YOUR INVESTING STRATEGY (EG.. 20% STOCKS, 50% COMMODITIES, 30% REAL ESTATE)

In today international marketplace, an investment portfolio that is well-maintained is essential to the success of any investors. As an investor, you have to know the way to figure out an asset that is suitable to your investment goals. Also, your portfolio has to fulfill your future needs and provide you with comfort and peace of mind. Portfolios must be aligned with goals and investment plans by following a detailed approach. Here are some steps you should follow when you're defining and creating your investment portfolio:

1. Determining the suitable asset allocation: determining your financial situations and goals is the first step in building a portfolio. Essential items to take into consideration are age, the amount of time you need to develop these investments, and the amount of capital needed to invest along with future needs. For example, a single graduate student just starting his career and a 70-year-old person who is married and wants to retire soon are going to have various investment plans.

2. Achieving the planned portfolio designed in the first step. When you have determined the correct asset allocation, you have to divide this capital among suitable asset classes. This isn't going to be difficult on a basic level where equities are going to be equities and bonds will be bonds. However, you can later on divide various asset classes into smaller categories or subclasses, which can have various risks and possible returns. Many investors choose to separate equity portions among various sectors, domestic, and international stocks. The portion of bonds could be allocated among them can be short or long term.

3. Re-evaluating portfolio weightings: when you have created a portfolio, you have to assess and rebalance it in a periodic manner

due to market movements, which can cause initial weightings to transform. To assess your portfolio's actual asset allocation, quantitatively categorize the investments and determine their values' proportion to the whole. Other factors that can change by time are the financial situation, potential needs, and tolerance for associated risks. When these things change, you are going to have to change or regulate your portfolio based on them. When the risk tolerance decreases, you are going to have to decrease the quantity of equities held. Also, you are going to have be ready to accept a greater risk and the allocation of your asset needs a smaller proportion of the assets to be placed in small caps stocks that are somewhat riskier.

4. Strategically rebalancing the portfolio. When you have determined the type of securities you want to decrease, and by which amount, you should decide the underweighted securities you will purchase with these proceeds. This also involves selling securities that are overweight or aren't leading to as much profits as expected. To select your securities, you should go for the second step. When you sell the assets to reassess your portfolio, you should time to take into consider tax implications associated with reassessing the portfolio. Perhaps the investment process is growth stocks have continuously appreciated during the previous year. In this situation, it could be beneficial not to contribute new funds to the class further one because this is going to

decreasing the weighting of the stocks in the portfolio by time with accumulating gains taxes.

THE FINAL LINE

Overall, a well-diversified portfolio is the best solution to ensure that your investments are continuously developing and growing on a long-term basis. This will also protect all your different assets from any risks of significant declines and different structural changes in the economy by time. Make sure that you regularly monitor the portfolio's diversification, make the necessary adjustments when it is needed, and you are going to enhance your opportunities of staying successful throughout their investment career.

CHAPTER 5 - PORTFOLIO BUILDING

After you have defined and created your investment portfolio, it is time for you to build on it and ensure that it is continuously successful. This chapter includes a detailed explanation of how to build on your portfolio, what a lazy portfolio is, and investing in different types of index ET along with its associated statistical advantages.

HOW TO BUILD A LAZY PORTFOLIO AND MAKE NICE PROFITS

Lazy portfolios are created to perform well in different market conditions. Most of them consist of a small amount of low-cost funds that can be easily being re-evaluated and re-balanced. The reason they are considered to be "lazy" is because investors can easily maintain the same asset allocation for extended time frames, because they general consist of thirty to forty percent bonds, and this percentage is suitable for many pre-retirement investors.

THREE FUND LAZY PORTFOLIOS

Three fund portfolios are one of the most important types of lazy portfolios and consist of three categories of bonds, total global market, and total American market. Also, you take in consideration that there are various close alternatives related to these funds, especially when buying them from Vanguards.

CORE FOUR PORTFOLIOS

One of the simplest methods to create a portfolio is by core and extended holdings. The core holdings make up most of portfolio's associated risk and return features. Also, extended holdings provide the last touches to any portfolio. The core four portfolio includes four different types of funds which make up the portfolio's 'cornerstone'. The chart below demonstrates how assets are allocated in core four portfolios.

INVESTING IN INDEX ETFs WITH STATISTICAL ADVANTAGES

Investing in ETF is another excellent choice and there are many options to choose from.

- **Vanguard Total Stock Market ETF**: It includes 34% of the overall stock portfolio and follows the CRSP U.S. Total Stock Market index. It covers all the American stock market and has 19% of its overall assets in medium sized organizations and 9% in smaller caps. When compared, the S&P 500 has 12% placed in mid caps and there is nothing placed in small funds. Just like the case with all funds explained in this book, stocks are usually weighted using market value. This can be calculated by multiplying shares prices with the amount of shares outstanding. Apple currently has the largest holding with 2.3% of the overall assets. The value of the average market of the holdings related to funds is $37 billion. The funds currently yield 1.9% of expenses and 0.05% every year.

- **Vanguard Total International Stock Index ETF**: this involves 22% of the overall stock portfolio and is the international twin of the Vanguard Total Stock Market ETF. It is reflected in the FTSE US Index where the average value of the market is about $21 billion. Markets that are somewhat developed account for about 86% of the overall assets of the funds and emerging markets make up the rest. Bigger companies take over the funds, but about 17% of it is in mid caps and 3% is placed in smaller caps. The ETD currently yields about 2.8% and charges about 0.14% every year.

- **Vanguard Dividend Appreciation Index ETF**: it includes 12% of the overall stock portfolio and involves only investing in companies that experienced an increase in its dividends during the last ten years. It follows the Nasdaq Dividend Achievers index, which eliminates companies that aren't financially strong, mainly because they have a lot of debt. Despite the focus of these dividends, it isn't considered to be a high yield, just 2.0% which is like the S&P 500. Also, dividend appreciation is considered to be an unusual index fund, but the reason it was included was due to growing proof that high quality stocks, especially blue chips that have attractive dividends, have performed greatly on a long-term basis. Also, yearly expenses account for 0.10%.

- **Vanguard Extended Market Index ETF**: it includes 12% of the overall stock portfolio and follows the S&P Completion index. It almost owns every tradable American public company, not including penny stocks or anything similar, that the S&P 500 currently doesn't own. Ever since 1926, the small caps have gone through an average of 2% yearly higher than somewhat larger companies, even though with higher volatility levels. Almost 6% of the ETF is currently invested in mid caps along with small caps and charges 0.10% yearly.

- **Vanguard Emerging Markets Stock Index ETF**: it includes 8% of the overall stock portfolio, follows the FTSE Emerging Markets index, which consists of 850 stocks from twenty-two different developing countries. Markets that are emerging have followed US stocks ineffectively since the end of 2011. However, this doesn't necessarily mean that economies that grow quickly don't deserve to be included in your long-term investments. This fund currently charges 0.15% every year. International stocks currently account thirty percent of assets, where 1/3 of them are emerging markets. During the last ten years in April 30, the investment portfolio returned a yearly 9.0%. By difference, the S&P 500 ended up returning a yearly 7.7% throughout the same stretch.

As far as investment vehicles are allocated, many investors should have about 70% to 75% of their investment portfolio placed in stock funds. However, it is recommended to decrease that as you start approaching retirement gradually. Even when retirement takes place, many individuals should try to keep 50% of their investments placed in stock funds.

CHAPTER 6 – PSYCHOLOGICAL ASPECTS

DON'T BELIEVE EVERYTHING ON CNBC OR IN A STOCK MARKET MAGAZINE

One of the main mistakes that many investors do, especially beginners, is that they follow what investing magazines or channels tell them to do. Yes, they do give great advice and recommendations, but this doesn't necessarily mean they are going to work for you as well.

TIME BRINGS SUCCESS!

Educating yourself is very important and this has become easy with the endless sources available. Many successful investors were able to teach themselves by reading and studying these sources. There are books, articles, videos, and websites, paid and for free, which you can use to understand all the different aspects related to investing. There is nothing wrong with seeking help. If you feel that there is something you are unable to understand and need further assistance in, there is nothing wrong with contacting investment professionals who will assist you in anything you need.

No one becomes successful or rich overnight and this is one of the main misconceptions many investors have once they start investing. One of things you should never do is take this as a get rich quick scheme. Investing is something that takes time, dedication, and really hard work. Patience is really important as well. If you try a certain strategy for example, and it doesn't work out, keep on trying until you get it right. Everything is difficult in the beginning and investing is no exception to this rule.

To be honest, buying stocks is not the difficult part. The challenge comes in when deciding which companies will benefit you - which are usually the companies that dominate the stock market consistently. This is where many prospective investors fall short and is why I've dedicated an entire chapter to choosing an investment plan.

The strategies that we're going to discuss in this chapter have been tried and tested countless times by numerous investors, and have been proven to work each time, without fail. Before I get started, here's one investment tip that could save your life: never invest more than 10% of your portfolio in individual stocks.

DON'T LET YOUR EMOTIONS GET THE BETTER OF YOU

Being successful in the stock market has nothing to do with your intellect, as we've said before. Instead, you need to be able to fight and control the urges that tend to get other investors into trouble when buying and selling stocks. You need to be able to think both logically and emotionally about your investments and be able to make your decision based on your head and your gut.

Overthinking an investment can also lead to disaster. You need to think hard about your investments, but not so hard that you start to second guess everything, causing you to miss out on what could have been an incredible opportunity. Likewise, overactivity in trading led by your emotions is one of the easiest ways to hinder your returns on your portfolio.

Being able to balance your logic and your emotions will help you in the long run.

CHOOSE COMPANIES RATHER THAN TICKER SYMBOLS

It can be difficult to remember that behind the jumble of letters and numbers of stock quotes found drifting along the bottom of a news broadcast is an actual company owned by real people. Try not to let the stock market and buying stock become an abstract concept in your mind. Remember that when you buy a share of a company, you are becoming a part-owner of that business.

You are going to encounter some overwhelming information that might cause an overload when you are on the hunt for potential business partners. Think of it this way: it is far easier to track down the right company when you're wearing a hat that says, 'I buy businesses.' You want to see how a business operates, its competitors, its place in the industry as a whole, whether it brings something new to your portfolio, and its prospects in the long term.

ALWAYS PLAN AHEAD

All investors, at some point or another, face the temptation to alter their relationship status with their stocks. As I mentioned earlier, making decisions in the heat of the moment can lead to the infamous investment blunder of buying high and selling low. This is where strategizing, and journaling comes in handy.

Try to write down some of the things that make all of the stocks in your portfolio worth committing to, and while you have a clear head, the situations that would justify ending your relationship with some stocks. Why are you buying, and why are you selling?

Write down exactly what about a certain company is appealing to you, and what opportunities you see it presenting in the future. Determine what your expectations are, what metrics matter the most, and the milestones that you will judge the progress of the company by. Organize the pitfalls that might occur and take note of the ones that might change the game completely, and which ones would only be a temporary setback.

Likewise, there can be many good reasons to decide to cut off an investment. For this part of your planning process, try to develop an investment prenup that clearly states what would cause you to let go of a stock. Do not confuse this with the movement of stock prices, especially not in the short term.

Rather focus on the changes that are fundamental to the business, and that would influence the company's ability to grow over the long term. If the company suddenly loses a major customer, or a major competitor enters the market, or the successor of the CEO moves the business toward a different direction, or your investment plan does not pan out after some time.

These are all things that might prompt you to sell a stock, but they are not the only reasons. You may have different, more personal reasons for letting go of an investment, all of which should be written down in your journal or business plan.

GRADUALLY BUILD UP YOUR POSITIONS

Time is the superpower of the investor, not timing. All of the most prosperous investors in the world buy stocks because they expect a reward from them, whether it comes from dividends or price appreciation over years or even decades. This means that you can take your time when buying as well. These are some strategies that can reduce your exposure to the volatility of price.

Buy in thirds

When you buy in thirds, you can avoid having your morale crushed by shaky results when you first start investing in the stock market. Divide the amount that you wish to invest by three, then pick three different points to buy shares, as the name suggests. These could either be based on company events and performance, or at regular intervals.

To give an example, you may decide to purchase shares before a product is released, and then put the next third of your money into these shares if it turns out to be a success. If it turns out to be a failure, you could divert the rest of your money elsewhere.

Dollar-cost average

While this may sound like a complex concept, it is quite plain. Dollar-cost averaging involves investing a predetermined sum of money at regular intervals, like once a month or every few months. This amount can buy more shares when the price of the stock decreases, and fewer shares when its price increases.

Overall, it evens out the average price that you'll end up paying. There are even a few online brokerage firms that allow investors to set up investing schedules that are entirely automated.

Buy 'the basket'

If you are not able to decide which one company out of a group in a certain industry will be the winner in the long term, you could just buy them all! Buying a basket of stocks will remove the pressure of having to pick 'the one' that will be successful. Having stakes in all of the competitors that meet your expectations means that you will not miss out if one of them turns out to be a hit.

You will be able to use the earnings from the winner company to offset any losses from the others that were not as successful. You'll also be able to identify which company is 'the one', allowing you to double down on your position if you wish.

STAY AWAY FROM OVERACTIVITY

You won't need to check up on your stocks more than once every quarter, like when you receive quarterly reports. Still, it can be tempting to monitor your stocks continually and see how they are performing, but doing so can lead to overreacting to minor events in the short term. It can also make you feel as though you need to do something when there's no need to act, and you end up focusing on the share price rather than the value of the company.

If and when one of your stocks goes through a sudden shift in price, try to figure out the cause. Has something changed business-wise for the company? Has your stock fallen victim to collateral damage caused by the market's response to an unrelated event? Or is it something that will influence your outlook on the long term in a meaningful way?

Short-term noise is very rarely relevant to how a well-chosen company will perform over the long term. Rather, it is how you, as an investor, reacts to the noise that truly matters. This is where your ability to think rationally and calmly comes into play, and when your investment plan will truly serve as a guide to holding out during the ebbs and flows of the stock market that are inevitable.

Evaluating a Stock

The reason that I consider stocks a long-term investment is because there is quite a lot of risk involved. You will need some time to weather any ebbs and flows and benefit from gains in the long term. Stock investment is great for generating money that you won't be desperately needing in the next five years.

Collect research materials for your stock

Before you invest in a stock, you'll want to review the financials of the associated company. This is what is known as quantitative research, and begins with gathering a couple of documents that companies are required to file with the Securities and Exchange Commission in the US.

Form 10-K

This form is an annual report that includes all of the independently audited key financial statements. This form allows you to review the company's source of income, its balance sheet, the way that it manages its income, and its expenses and revenues.

Form 10-Q

This form is much more straightforward. It is merely a quarterly update on the company's financial results and its operations.

If you are short on time, you can always find highlights from the forms mentioned above and other essential financial ratios on the website of your brokerage firm, or on major financial news sites. This information is crucial, as it lets you compare the performance of one company against its competitors and other candidates for your investment.

TIGHTEN YOUR FOCUS

The financial reports mentioned above contain dozens upon dozens of numbers and values, and it is very easy to become overwhelmed. That's why it is so important to focus on certain terms so that you can familiarize yourself with the inner workings of a measurable company.

Net Income

The net income of a company is called its *bottom-line* figure, since it is listed at the end of an income statement. Very creative. It is the total sum of money that a company is made after its operating expenses, depreciation and taxes have been deducted from the revenue. Revenue is the equivalent of your gross salary, while net income can be seen as what money you have left over after you have paid your taxes and rent.

Revenue

Revenue is the amount of cash that a company brings in during a specified period. It is the first thing you will see on an income statement and is thus referred to as the *top line* figure. Revenue can sometimes be categorized into *operating revenue* and *non-operating revenue.* Operating revenue is usually the most informative since it is generated from the core business of the company. Non-operating revenue usually comes from once-off business activities, like when an asset is sold.

Price-Earnings Ratio (P/E)

To determine the trailing P/E ratio of a company, you need to divide its current stock price by its earnings per share, generally over the last year. On the other hand, when you divide the stock price by the earnings predicted by Wall Street analysts, you're able to see the forward P/E of a company. This measure of the value of a stock can help you determine how much investors are willing to pay to receive $1 of a company's earnings.

Remember that the P/E ratio is divided from the earnings per share calculation that can potentially be flawed and estimates from analysts are usually focused on the short term. This means that it is not a very reliable metric on its own.

Earnings and Earnings Per Share (EPS)

Dividing a company's earnings by the number of available shares for trade, you receive the earnings per share. This value indicates how profitable a company is based on per-share, making it far easier to compare with other competitor companies. When you notice that earnings per share value is followed by '(ttm)', it is referring to the 'trailing twelve months'.

This measurement is not even close to perfect since it does not indicate how efficiently a company is making use of its capital. Some companies will take their earnings and pay them out to shareholders in dividends, while others might use them to reinvest in the business.

Return on Assets (ROA) and Return on Equity (ROE)

In terms of percentiles, the return on equity of a company reveals how much profit it is generating with each dollar that is invested by shareholders. The equity belongs to the shareholders. On the other hand, return on assets is an indication of the percentage of profits that a company makes with each dollar of its assets. Each of these values is determined by dividing the company's net annual income by one of the above measures.

These percentages will also inform you about how efficiently a company is making profits. You will need to be wary of the 'gotchas' here. A company can boost its return on equity artificially by buying shares back, thereby reducing the shareholder equity denominator. Likewise, taking on more debt, like taking more loans to finance property or increase inventory, will add to the amount in assets used to calculate return on assets.

This is plenty of information to absorb, and it's perfectly normal to feel slightly overwhelmed. Do your best to take in what we've stated above so that you'll be ready for the next chapter, in which we're going to discuss the process of making your first stock investment!

CHAPTER 7 – THE FIRST INVESTMENT

Unfortunately, investing in the stock market is not as simple as going to a store to make a purchase. The process of buying stocks involves creating a brokerage account, adding funds, and doing your homework about which stocks you should buy before tapping the purchase button on your broker's app or website.

This chapter discusses all of the steps you need to take before buying your first stock, as well as how you should go about choosing stocks that are worth your time and money.

FIND AN ONLINE BROKER THAT WORKS FOR YOU

The method for choosing an online broker that suits you the best has changed slightly over the years. Most major brokers nowadays have eliminated commissions for trading, which results in cost being largely out of the question. This leaves you with two primary considerations when comparing brokers.

You need to think about if a broker is meeting your needs and requirements, and how easy it is for you to use their platform. The latter is sometimes more important, especially as a newer investor, as it makes entering the field more accessible.

Is your broker providing all you need?

An example of a good online broker would be one that offers some great learning resources for newer investors, stock research, and some other tools. Certain online brokers also offer face-to-face branches, for those who decide that they want some guidance in person.

Other notable features that could be beneficial include allowing investors to trade in foreign markets and allowing them to buy fractional stock shares. Not all brokers provide these features, so try to look out for the ones that do.

Is the platform easy to navigate and user-friendly?

Like I said earlier, this question is probably slightly more important for new investors, as jumping into a complex trading platform can be confusing and will often leave you feeling demotivated. If you decide that you are going to trade from your phone or tablet, you will want a mobile broker platform that is user-friendly enough for you.

Luckily, most of the popular brokers let you test their trading platforms out with virtual money before you sign up. This allows you to try a few out before deciding on one platform to trade with.

OPEN YOUR BROKERAGE ACCOUNT, AND FUND IT

Once you have decided on a brokerage platform, you will need to complete a new account application. You will want to have your Social Security number and driver's license on hand, and your bank account details as well if you are going to fund your account from your personal savings account.

The sign-up process is generally quick and painless, and you'll have to make two decisions when completing an application.

Are you looking for options trading privileges?

As a new investor, it is better to stay away from options until you know what you are doing, and you are familiar with the stock market. There are generally a variety of options privileges that you can choose from, and you always have the option to apply for a change later on.

Are you looking for margin privileges?

Margin privileges essentially allow you to borrow money to use for buying more stocks. Even though investing on margin is not ideal, having margin privileges can be beneficial sometimes. You usually are not able to use deposited funds until they are cleared, unless you have a margin account.

When it comes to funding your account, there are a few options available to you. Most people choose to use EFT, or electronic funds transfer, to deposit money into their account. Other common methods include wiring the money or mailing the brokerage a check.

DECIDE ON STOCKS TO BUY

We've already talked about analyzing stocks and classifying them in the previous chapters, so, with that information in mind, it's time to determine which stock or stocks you want to buy into your new account. Remember to concentrate on the long term and acquire stock that you want to own for the next five or ten years. Do not only focus on stocks that you think will perform well in the next couple of months.

You also need to keep in mind how beneficial diversification is. You don't want to put all of your cash in only three or four stocks, even if you are starting your account with a small sum of money. Since trading has become mostly free of commissions, it is now more practical to purchase a couple of shares in several different stocks.

CHOOSE AN ORDER TYPE

You will have a few different types of orders to choose from, with 'market' orders being the best choice for investors looking at the long term. This lets you brokerage know that you wish to buy stocks right away, and at the best price possible.

Another pretty common type of order is called a 'limit' order. With this type of order, the broker knows the highest price that you are willing to pay. To give an example, you might want a stock that is currently trading for $22 per share, but you want to be able to buy it for less than $20. So, you're able to enter a limit order that tells your broker only to purchase if the price reaches a level that you desire.

After you have filled out your trade ticket and have pressed 'place order', it should take mere seconds for your broker to execute the order. Once that is done, the shares should show up on your account straight away.

ENTER YOUR ORDERS

This is the final step in the process of buying your first stocks. You will need to place the order with your broker by entering the stock symbol of your choice, whether you are buying or selling shares, and the number of shares you want.

Then, all you need to do is observe as the long-term compounding ability of the market does all the work for you. You can usually enroll in the DRIP plan of your broker with the press of a button if you want your dividends to be reinvested into more shares automatically.

Like I said before, try not to check up on your stocks too often, as tempting as it may be. Of course, you should keep up to date with the latest news from your companies by subscribing to news and looking at the quarterly reports. Just don't panic and sell if your stocks go down slightly.

Likewise, if your stocks increase slightly, try not to cash out right away. The best way to accumulate wealth over a long period is to buy shares from good companies and keep them for as long as those companies are successful.

Now that we've gone over how to make your first investment, let's look at some of the stocks you can expect to find on the market:

VALUE STOCKS

In the stock market, the idea of value investing is the belief that if you can analyze the finances of enough companies and fairly predict the prices of stocks, you will be able to find stocks that are undervalued and might make attractive investments. This approach was first developed by the famous British economist, Benjamin Graham.

Value investing is what made many successful investors wealthy, but it is not always easy to find undervalued stocks. An incredibly useful measurement is to look at a company's book value per share, which details the assets of a company in comparison to the current share price.

You will want to be extra careful when it comes to smaller businesses, since they are almost always riskier and more prone to volatility than other stocks with a more stable value. You should also be wary of any companies that have experienced a major shift in price recently, because such shifts and any news events associated with them may influence several valuation and ratio methods.

BLUE-CHIP STOCKS

Blue-chip stocks refer to those that are part of companies that are not likely to be influenced by major negative news stories, and that are longtime market standbys. Even if they were to be faced with negative publicity, they are companies that are old enough and sturdy enough to bounce back without any hindrances.

Blue chips are excellent for new investors since they will usually shift predictably with the market, and are not at as much of a risk than most other stocks. Walmart is an excellent example of a blue-chip stock. They are a chain store with a history dating back to 1962, have a massive market cap of $339.72 billion, and are relatively stable in comparison to the market as a whole.

The company holds the number one spot on the Fortune 500 list as of 2019, with more than $500 billion in annual revenue. The Fortune 500, and other lists like it, are excellent places for new investors to track down blue-chip investments.

Below is a checklist for buying your first stock:

1. *Buy what you know*

2. *Understand how the company makes money*

3. *Understand how the company is measuring its growth*

4. *Recognize the risk factors and competition*

5. *Understand how the company is spending its free cash flow*

6. *See if the stock is cheap in relation to its peers and the market*

CHAPTER 8:
PROFITS, PROFITS, PROFITS!

You do not need to be hitting home runs to be successful in the stock market. Instead, you should focus on getting the base hits, and try to grow your portfolio by taking most gains in the range of 20%-25%. While it may sound counterintuitive, it is always best to sell stock when it's on the rise, consistently advancing and looking appealing to all other investors.

As you may have already figured out, trading on the stock market is a risky business, though the rewards that can come from these risks make it all worth it. Even though you will never be able to eliminate the risks completely, there are some things you can do to mitigate risks by actively managing your portfolio and making smart investments.

However, if you are not careful, or if you don't really know what you're doing, you could end up paying a pretty hefty price. The buy low and sell high strategy might have resulted in the success of many investors, but it is not how the real professionals become successful. Instead, smart investors deploy their money strategically in order to allow it to work in more ways than one. In layman's terms, they multitask their money.

In this chapter, we're going to look at some of the ways you can maximize your profits and get the most out of your investments.

PRICE ACTION STRATEGIES

If you were to think of investing like a game, the way you would win would be to purchase a stock at a low price and then sell it later on at a higher price. If you are a homeowner, then you likely understand this concept quite practically. It's best to use one of two strategies to make a profit on your investment.

The first is known as **value investing**, which relates to the **value stocks** mentioned in the previous chapter. Like the products you buy from stores each and every day, stocks go on sale every now and then, and value investors wait for this sale to happen. This makes it easier for them to make a profit, since stocks that are undervalued, or *on sale,* have more room for growth.

Unfortunately, your favorite stock might not be suited to this strategy since it has to pay a dividend. It would need to have a price low enough for you to be able to buy 100 shares, and it needs to trade many shares every day - at least 1 million shares of daily volume is preferable. Keep in mind that the value of a company is not based on its price.

There are many high-quality stocks that trade for $100 or more, and stocks that cost between $15 and $30, with a dividend yield of at least 2%, are the most favorable. You also want to avoid stocks that are highly volatile, as their more unpredictable shifts in price are more difficult to manage. This is where your stock evaluation skills and research will be put to the test.

Once you have found your stock, and you have decided that you want to value invest, you want this name to be in the middle or near the bottom of the trading range for the last 52 weeks. If it is not currently there, then you should either find another company or just wait for the stock to be at a price you are willing to pay for.

The second strategy is known as **momentum trading.** Some investors believe that the best time for a stock to be bought is when it's price continues to rise, since, as we learned in school, objects in motion tend to remain in motion. The only problem with this strategy is that it is usually only beneficial to short-term investors. Most people want to think of the long term, as the longer you are in possession of stock, the better its potential returns can be.

INVEST FOR DIVIDENDS

In the world of high-tech stock trading, it is often considered boring to invest for dividends, but they can truly be a major source of income for long-term investors. Dividends provide us with two distinct advantages that help us get our money working in more ways than one. First, they provide a stable income. Even though companies may choose to pay or not to pay dividends, companies of higher qualities and with lower payout ratios have a lower chance of cutting your quarterly dividend payment.

Let's use an example to put things into perspective. You've done your research and have decided to buy shares in stock *XYZ*. You purchased 100 shares at $30 each, which had a 3% dividend yield at the time.

$$\$3\,000 \times 3\% = \$90 \text{annually}$$

You are not only making $90 every year, but because a dividend is paid to your account as cash, you can apply that payment of dividends to what you paid for the stock for each year you own the 100 shares. In this case, you can also subtract 90 cents per share. After only five years, the stock that once cost you $30 per share will go down to $25.50 per share. Many long-term investors are able to reduce the price that they paid for stock to $0 from the dividend alone.

MAKE USE OF COVERED CALLS

Covered calls are slightly more complex. If you are not confident with this kind of strategy, using the method of purchasing a stock and collecting its dividend as it increases will still provide you with some significant gains. You need to ask yourself two important questions before you sell a covered call:

What is the strike price?

Strike price

Covered calls are a kind of options contract strategy that allows the contract holder to purchase your 100 shares, if it is at the strike price or above it. You probably do not want someone to take your shares from you, though you might have a change of heart later in your career, so the strike price will need to be steep enough that the stock does not rise above it, but low enough that you will still be able to collect a decent premium for taking a risk.

This is a pretty tough decision to make, especially for new investors such as yourself. If your stock is currently experiencing a downtrend, you will likely be able to sell an option with a strike price not much higher than the current actual price of the stock. If the stock is experiencing an uptrend, however, you may want to wait until you are happy that the move up has run its course, and that the stock will soon shift in the opposite direction. Remember that whenever a stock appreciates in value, your option value depreciates.

Expiration date

The further you take your option into the future, the bigger your premium payout will be upfront, to sell the call, but that also means more time that your stock needs to be below the strike price, to avoid it being 'called away' from you. Consider going three or four months ahead for your first contract.

As soon as you sell it, your covered call will make money for you, since the premium that is paid by the buyer will be deposited into your account directly. It will keep making money for you even if your stock's price drops. The premium falls with the price. You are able to buy back the contract from the buyer at any time, so, if the premium does fall, you can buy it for less than what you sold it for.

That means you're making a profit. At the same time, if your stock were to rise above the strike price, you would be able to buy the contract for more than you sold it, causing a loss, but also saving you needing to hand over 100 of your shares. One of the most effective ways to use the covered call is to collect the premium right at the beginning.

Even though you can buy the option back if its price shifts, you will want to only do so under dire circumstances. You should also keep in mind that the money you collect from selling your covered call can also be deducted from the price you paid for the stock.

The easiest way to get the hang of a new investment strategy is to make use of a virtual platform, like the ones many brokerage firms offer in their apps or websites. You are still able to buy the stock and collect dividends but wait to sell the covered call until you feel that you are comfortable with the way it works.

CHAPTER 9:
KNOWING WHEN TO SELL

The money-making process with stocks involves two crucial decisions - knowing when it's the right time to buy, and when it's the right time to sell. You have to have both of them right to be able to make profits. Generally, there are three good reasons as to why you should sell a stock:

1. **The price of the stock has increased drastically**

2. **The stock has reached a price that is no longer sustainable**

3. **Buying the stock in the first place was a mistake**

In this chapter, we are going to look at these reasons in more detail and discuss their implications.

BUYING RIGHT

The first thing used to determine the return on any investment is its purchase price. You could argue that a loss or profit is made the second that it is purchased - the buyer just won't know until it has been sold. Even though buying at the correct price might determine the profit made in the end, selling at the right price will *guarantee* that a profit is made. If you do not sell at the correct time, the benefits you had from buying at the right time could fall away.

SELLING STOCK IS DIFFICULT

Many investors have a hard time selling stocks, and it has a lot to do with our greedy nature as humans. Let's give a common scenario:

You purchase a share of stocks for $25, and intend to sell it, if and when it reaches $30. It hits $30, so you then decide to wait a bit longer for a few more points. The stock then reaches $33, and soon your greed overpowers your ability to think rationally. Suddenly, the price of the stock drops down to $28, and you tell yourself to wait again until it's back at $30. This will never happen, and you will finally give in to your frustrations and sell it when it drops to $24.

Greed and emotion can very easily overcome your rational thinking, as you can see. You will have treated the stock market the same way you would a slot machine and lost. To remove human error from the equation for future decisions, try using a limit order, which will sell the stock automatically once it has reached your target price. You won't even need to monitor the performance of that stock - you'll just receive a notification when the sell order is placed.

WHEN THE PURCHASE WAS A MISTAKE

If you are a diligent investor, you probably did some research into a stock before you bought it. At a later stage, you might realize that you had made an analytical error that affects the suitability for a business as an investment in a fundamental way. You should then sell the stock, even if it has to be at a loss.

The key to being a successful investor is to rely on your analysis and data rather than the emotional mood swings of the stock market. If your analysis, for any reason, turns out to be flawed, sell the stock and move forward. The price of the stock could increase after you've sold it, which can make you second guess yourself. Or a 10% loss on that particular investment might be the smartest decision you have ever made.

Obviously, not all analytical errors are the same. If a business does not meet your predictions for the short term, and the price of the stock decreases, do not overreact and sell if the integrity of the business remains the same. However, if you do notice that the company is losing market share to its competitors, it could be a sign of weakness in the long term and would constitute a good reason to sell.

WHEN THE STOCK EXPERIENCES A DRASTIC RISE

It is not impossible for your stock to rise significantly in a short period for any number of reasons. The best investors are those that are the most humble. Do not assume that a rise is an affirmation that you are smarter than the market itself. Instead, sell.

Cheap stocks can become expensive stocks very quickly for a wide variety of reasons, including the speculation of others. Rather take your gains and move on. Even better, if a stock suddenly drops, consider buying it again.

SELL FOR VALUATION

This decision for selling is part scientific, part artistic. Ultimately, the value of a stock rests on the current value of the future cash flows of a company. Since the future is uncertain, the valuation will always be, to some extent, imprecise. This is why the majority of value investors very heavily rely on the margin of safety concepts when investing.

It is generally always a good idea to consider selling if the valuation of a company reaches a significantly higher level than that of its peers. This rule does have many exceptions, though, which is what makes it so complex. For example, if *Company A* is trading for 15 times earnings, and *Company B* is trading for 13 times earnings, then there is no reason that you should not sell *Company A* when considering the sizable market share of their products.

Another selling tool that is slightly more reasonable is to sell when the P/E ratio of a company exceeds its own average P/E ratio for the last 7-10 years significantly. To give another example, Walmart shares had a 60 times earnings P/E at the height of the internet boom. Despite the quality of the company, any investors who owned shares in Walmart should have and could have considered selling, and prospective buyers should have thought of looking elsewhere.

When the revenue of a company drops, it is usually an indication that the demand has decreased. You should first look at the annual revenue figure in order to get a look at the bigger picture, but you should not rely on these numbers alone. Take a look at the quarterly figures too. The numbers of annual revenue for a major gas and oil company could be impressive on an annual basis, but what if energy prices have dropped in the last few months?

When you notice that a company is cutting costs, it usually means that said company is not thriving. The most telling indicator for this is a reduced headcount. The good news, for you at least, is that initially, cutting costs will be seen as a positive, which tends to lead to stock gains. Though you should not view this as an opportunity to acquire more shares, but instead as a way to leave the position before the inevitable plummet in value.

SELLING BECAUSE OF FINANCIAL REQUIREMENTS

This reason may not be 'valid' from an analytical point of view, but it is still a reason. Stocks are, at the end of the day, assets, and there are sometimes where people will have to cash in on their assets. Whether the money will be used as capital for a new business, purchasing a new home, or paying for college tuition, the decision is entirely dependent on your financial situation, rather than the fundamentals of the stock market.

REBALANCING YOUR PORTFOLIO

Sometimes, you may decide that your portfolio is not diverse in the way that you wish it were. This is a perfectly valid reason to sell a stock or several stocks, and there are two situations where this could be a necessity.

Reducing stock exposure

As you grow older and draw closer to your retirement, it is a good idea to reduce your stock exposure gradually. Even though stocks do have great potential for returns in the long term, they are, as you know, quite volatile, and preservation of capital becomes more and more important as you get closer to retiring.

One good rule is to subtract your current age from 110 to get the percentage of your current portfolio that you should invest in the stock market. If it's been a couple of years since the last time you adjusted your allocation of assets, it may be a good thought to sell some of your holdings in stocks and put the money into bonds.

High-performance stocks

Sometimes, your stocks perform well. Very well. So well, in fact, that it seems unreasonable to have so much money invested in a single company. In this case, it is a good idea to sell, so that the wealth of your portfolio can be distributed more evenly across more companies.

THE COMPANY HAS BEEN ACQUIRED

When the acquisition of a company is announced, the price for the stocks of the company being acquired will usually rise to a level that is similar to the agreed-upon price. Nine times out of ten, it is a wise idea to lock in your gains, as the upside potential is usually pretty limited. There are three ways that a company can be potentially acquired -stock, cash, or both.

In a cash-only acquisition, the stock will usually move toward the price of acquisition. It is rarely worth holding onto your shares in this type of acquisition, as there is no real upside for having your money tied up for months, and if the deal were to collapse, your shares could plummet.

With stock or cash-and-stock acquisition, it can be slightly more complex, and your decision will have to come down to whether or not you want to be a shareholder in the company that is making the acquisition. If not, it is perfectly reasonable to cash out.

In the next chapter, we're going to look at how you should be managing your stock portfolio as a new investor and some of the things you can do to make managing your investment portfolio easier and more efficient.

CHAPTER 10:
MANAGING YOUR STOCK PORTFOLIO

Too many young people very rarely invest for retirement, if ever. Some far away date, like 40 or 50 years into the future, is difficult for many new, young investors to comprehend. But, without investments to supplement income during retirement, if you have any at all, prospective investors will likely find it difficult to make it pay for the necessities.

Investments that are disciplined, smart, and made on a regular basis in a portfolio with holdings that are diverse can yield some great returns in the long term. One of the primary reasons that young people do not invest is that they do not understand stocks fully or fail to wrap their heads around basic concepts like the power of compounding and the time value of money. Luckily, these things are not difficult to learn, and you're holding in your hands the best resource out there to learn them.

You need to start investing early. The sooner you start, the more time that your investments will have to grow and compound. Most of the investment industry involves making things sound more complicated than they are so that you feel inadequate enough to let an 'expert' control your money.

Of course, trustworthy advice from an advisor with a good reputation will always be useful, the simple truth is that paying exorbitant prices for professional investment management will not automatically guarantee superior investment return, especially once you have your fees accounted for. Proactive investors who want to take their destiny into their own hands will be glad to hear that it is not very difficult at all to build a portfolio and manage it using the same techniques that the pros do.

Let's look at how you should manage your investment portfolio.

Learn Some Simple Principles of Investing

As you may have learned from *Chapter Two,* there are a wide variety of investment strategies out there, and some of them can be quite daunting and intimidating. Even though using a complication system that requires plenty of attention, information, and time might work perfectly well for some folks, they are not needed to be a successful investor. Using one of the strategies that was mentioned in *Chapter Two* will be more than adequate, since they are not very complicated, but are still super effective.

Start Early

As soon as you start working and earning money, you should begin saving by participating in a 401(k) retirement plan, if your employer offers it. If there is no 401(k) available, establish an IRA, or Individual Retirement Account and earmark a percentage of your compensation for a contribution to your account each month. Creating an automatic cash contribution that goes off each month is a very convenient and efficient way to save a 401(k) or IRA.

Try to remember that savings accumulate, and your interest will compound without taxes only for so long as you do not withdraw the money. This means that it would be wise to establish one of these investment vehicles early in your working career.

EARLY HIGHER RISK ALLOCATION

Another good reason to start saving your money early is that the younger you are, the less likely it is for you to become burdened with financial obligations, like children, a spouse, or a mortgage, to name but a few. Without these burdens in your life, you are able to allocate some of your investment portfolio to investments that have a higher risk, which will often return greater yields.

Also, when you begin investing as a young person, before you start accumulating financial commitments, you will likely have more cash available to invest, and a much greater period of time before your retirement. You will have a greater retirement *nest egg* with more money to invest, for years and years to come.

EXEMPLARY EGGS

Let's illustrate the advantage of investing as soon as you are able. Assume that, every month, you invest $200 from the age of 25. If you are earning an annual return on that money of 7%, when you reach the age of 65, your retirement nest egg is going to be somewhere around $525,000.

However, if you only start saving that $200 each month when you are 35 years old, and still receive the same return of 7%, then you will only have about

$244,000 when you are 65 years old. For those who start investing only later in their lives, there are some tax advantages available. Notably, 401(k) plans allow for *catch-up contributions* for folks that are 50 years and older. IRAs do this as well.

DIVERSIFY

You've read it time and time again throughout this guide, but you should always select stocks across a wide range of market categories. The most effective way to do this is via an index fund. You should try to invest in stocks that are conservative, and have regular dividends, as well as stocks that have a potential to grow in the long term, and a small number of stocks that have a better risk potential or can provide better returns.

If you are investing in stocks individually, avoid putting more than 4% of your total portfolio into one stock. This will prevent your portfolio from being affected adversely if one or two stocks suffer a drastic downturn. Some AAA-rated bonds can also be excellent investments for the long term, either government or corporate.

KEEP YOUR COSTS AS LOW AS POSSIBLE

It is always a good idea to invest with a discount brokerage firm. Another reason for you to consider index funds as a new investor is that their fees are usually quite low. Since you are (probably) going to be investing for the long term, you should do your best to avoid buying and selling regularly in response to short term market ups and downs. This will save you some expenses for commission and management fees, which might prevent losses in cash when your stock price declines.

INVESTING REGULARLY AND BEING DISCIPLINE

Ensure that you are putting your money into your investments regularly and in a disciplined manner. This might not be possible if you were to become unemployed, but once you have secured another job, you will be able to continue to fund your portfolio.

TAKE YOUR TIME

You do not need to rush when selecting a portfolio or implementing one. When you have settled on a portfolio that you are happy with, sleep on it before making any other decisions. In fact, you should wait at least a few months before making another move. Buyer's remorse is totally normal when you are returning an item to a store, but exchanging a portfolio has some major implications when it comes to tax. You will need to be clever about your decisions and to act with as little emotion as possible.

When you are just entering the stock market industry, you should try not to stress about having your portfolio implemented perfectly right away. A good way to start any portfolio would be to buy a large cap index fund or a total stock market, since it will act as a main component for pretty much all other asset allocations that you grow into.

As you accumulate more money and become more educated as to the inner workings of the stock market, you will be able to look at newer, more exciting assets and diversify your holdings and move towards an asset allocation goal set in the long term.

REBALANCE EVERY YEAR

The best way you could manage your portfolio is to ignore it, despite the impression that you might be getting from financial news outlets. Keep in mind that you are already much better off than many other investors, since you have already decided on an asset allocation, and are paying close attention to its volatility and returns historically. You can rest easy knowing that you have made a well-educated decision.

Markets fluctuate constantly, and your allocation of assets will do its job passively, while also growing and protecting your money without you needing to monitor it constantly. However, you will need to check up on your money once a year to see if any of your assets have shifted from your target percentages.

If they have, then you are going to need to rebalance. There are two ways in which you can do this. The first is to use new money that you have accumulated and saved over the year and purchase shares of the funds that have dipped below the price you were aiming for. Alternatively, you could sell the shares of the funds that performed the best and use the money to acquire more shares of those that did not.

ABOUT TAXES

You should always remember that if you are investing in an account that can be taxed, so one that is not a 401(k) or an IRA, then selling funds is going to impact your taxes. I recommend buying shares with new money first before you sell anything. When you do have to sell, make sure that you understand the tax implications of any change before it is made.

This may sound quite daunting, but think of it positively. There are many ways that you can reduce tax by managing your own portfolio smartly, in ways that other investors who are giving their portfolio choices to others are not able to. If you are still confused, it may be beneficial to see a tax advisor. However, once you have gone through the process once or twice, you will get the hang of it in no time.

LIFE GOES ON

It's really as simple as finding an appropriate portfolio that suits you, purchasing the index funds that you need from a brokerage account, and rebalancing once every year. You have complete control over your portfolio, and you certainly have the ability to manage it using the methods for asset allocation from respected experts. It's much easier than it sounds.

CHAPTER 11:
ANALYZING THE MARKET

You're never asked to be your own lawyer or doctor, so why should you be obligated to be your own stock market analyst? Some people take up cooking merely because it is something that they enjoy. Likewise, there are folks who enjoy the process of making investments. Therefore, if you are the type of investor that enjoys being independent and self-reliant, then you should certainly consider becoming your own stock analyst.

Some analysts have a question mark hovering over their credibility rating, so it is always better to get the hang of analysis on your own. That's what we'll be discussing in this chapter.

TRUST THE STOCK ANALYSIS PROCESS

Regardless of whether you are an investor looking for value or growth, developing your mind is the first step you need to take toward thinking like an analyst. You need to figure out what to sell and what to buy, and at what price. Analysts will generally focus on a certain sector or industry. Within that industry, they'll focus on a certain few companies.

The goal of an analyst is to deeply inspect the affairs of each of the companies on their list. This is done by analyzing their financial statements and all other information from the company that they can get their hands on. In order to cross-examine the facts, analysts will also inspect the companies' suppliers, competitors, and customers, and their affairs.

Some analysts will also visit a company and interact with its management so that they can understand first-hand of the company. Over time, professional analysts will connect all the dots to get a good view of the bigger picture. Before you make any sort of investment, you need to do your own research. It's always more beneficial to research into several stocks of the same industry so that your analysis can be comparative.

Accessing this information generally is not a problem. The biggest issue that you might face when trying to become your own stock market analyst is time. Retail investors who are busy with a number of other projects at once might not be able to allocate as much time as a professional security analyst might.

But, you are definitely able to take just a couple of firms from the start, to test how well you are able to analyze them. Doing so will help you understand the process, and, with more time and experience, you can think about inspecting and analyzing more and more stocks.

START WHERE YOU ARE

The best way to start your own analysis is to look over other analyst reports. That way, you can save much more time by cutting down the amount of preliminary work you need to do. You do not need to buy or follow the recommendations that other analysts make blindly. Instead, you should read their research reports so that you can have a quick overview of the company, including its main competitors, strengths, weaknesses, future prospects, and industry outlook.

Analyst reports are packed full of useful information, and reading these reports made by various analysts at the same time will help you identify any similarities. Opinions might vary, but the basic facts in all of the reports should be common. Additionally, you can also look more closely at the earnings forecasts that different analysts create, which ultimately determine their buy and sell recommendations.

Different analysts might set different target prices for the same stock. You should always look for the reasons while you are studying the analyst reports. What would have *your* opinion been regarding the current stock given the same information? No idea? Look at the next heading.

WHAT SHOULD YOU ANALYZE?

You are going to have to understand the various steps involved in the process of stock analysis if you want to arrive at your own reliable conclusion about a stock. Some analysts will use the *top-down* strategy, starting with a certain industry, then locating a winning company. Others will follow a *bottom-up* approach, in which they start with a particular company and then inspect the outlook of the industry. You do not need to use any of these strategies, and you are at liberty to create your own order, so long as the entire process flows smoothly.

ANALYZING AN INDUSTRY

There are sources available to the public for almost any industry. The annual report of a company itself often provides a good enough overview of the industry that it belongs to, along with its predictions for growth in the future. Annual reports can also provide some information about the minor and major competitors in any particular industry.

Reading the reports from two or three companies at the same time will usually give you a clear picture. You could also subscribe to websites and trade magazines that cater to a certain industry for monitoring the latest events in that industry.

ANALYZING BUSINESS MODELS

You need to be able to determine the strengths and weaknesses of a company and be able to focus on them. There can be a weak company in a strong industry, and a strong company in a weak industry. A company's strengths are usually reflected in things like its products, suppliers, customers, and unique brand identity. You can learn about the business model of a company from its annual report, websites, and trade magazines.

FINANCIAL STRENGTH

Understanding a company's financial strength is the most crucial step to analyzing a stock, whether you like it or not. Without being able to understand the financials, you are not going to be able to think like an analyst. You should be able to understand a company's income statement, balance sheet, and cash flow statements.

Usually, the figures lying in the financial statements are more meaningful than the glossy words written in an annual report. If you are not comfortable with numbers, but you want to be able to analyze stocks, then there is no time like right now to start familiarizing yourself with them.

QUALITY OF MANAGEMENT

This is another crucial factor for any stock analyst. You may have heard that there are no good or bad companies, but only good or bad managers - the key executives that are responsible for the future of the company. You can assess the management of a company and the quality of its board by doing a bit of research on the internet. There is a multitude of information out there about every public company.

ANALYSIS OF GROWTH

Stock prices follow earnings, so if you want to know whether the price of a stock is going to move upward or downward in the future, then you will need to know where the future earnings are going. Unfortunately, there is no simple formula that you will be able to use to know what to expect for future earnings. Analysts generally make their own estimates by looking at the past figures for growth of sales and profit margins, as well as a particular industry's profitability trends.

Essentially, it connects what has occurred in the past to what is predicted to happen in the future. If you are able to make earnings forecasts that are accurate enough, you will be able to assess your abilities as a stock analyst, since it is a clear indication of your understanding of those companies and industries.

CHAPTER 12:
MISTAKES TO AVOID

Failure is a part of the learning process of investing and trading. As an investor, you will usually be involved in holdings in the long term and will trade in stocks, other securities, and exchange-traded funds. Traders usually sell and buy future options, are involved in a higher number of transactions, and hold their positions for shorter periods.

Even though investors and traders make use of two different kinds of trading transactions, they are often responsible for making nearly identical mistakes. Some of these mistakes can be more detrimental to investors, while others can be more detrimental to traders. Both traders and investors will be better off to remember these common mistakes and how they can be avoided.

FAILING TO PLAN

Every experienced trader enters the industry with a plan that has been carefully thought out. They know their exact points of exit and entry, the maximum loss that they are willing to take, and the amount of capital that they need to invest in the trade. Beginner traders might not have a plan to follow before they begin trading.

Even if they do have a plan, they might still be more likely to shift away from their established plan than more experienced traders would. Novice traders might even change their course completely. For example, you might go short after you had initially bought securities since the share price is dropping, and only end up being whipsawed.

CLUTCHING PERFORMANCE

Numerous traders and investors will choose strategies, classes, funds, and managers based on a relevant strong performance. The feeling of missing out on returns has likely led to more bad investment decisions than most other investment factors. If a certain strategy, asset class, or fund has performed very well for four or five years, you can know one thing for sure: you should have invested four or five years ago. Now, the specific cycle that caused that good performance is probably drawing to a close. The smart money is heading out.

NOT REGAINING BALANCE

As we discussed in a previous chapter, the process of getting your portfolio back to its desired allocation of assets, as outlined in your investment plan, is known as rebalancing. Rebalancing can be difficult since it might force you to sell the asset class that is doing the best and buy more assets from a class that is not performing well.

This contrarian action is quite challenging for many new investors. However, portfolios that are left to drift with the market return will guarantee that asset classes will be overweight at market peaks and underweight at the lows of the market - a recipe for bad performance. Rebalance religiously and receive the rewards in the long term.

IGNORING AVERSIONS TO RISK

You have to continually keep track of your risk tolerance, or the capacity you have to take risks. Many investors can't handle the ups and downs and volatility that is linked to the stock market or other trades that are more speculative. Other investors might need a secure source of regular interest income. These investors with a low tolerance for risk will be well off investing in the blue-chip stocks from established businesses rather than the more volatile startup and growth company shares.

Always keep in mind that any investment return has a risk attached to it. The investments with the lowest risk are those in US treasury bills, bonds, and notes. There are many types of investments from there that move up the ladder of risk and can also offer greater returns as compensation for the higher risk that they make you take on.

If an investment offers a very appealing return, you should also inspect the risk profile that is attached to it and how much money you might lose if things were to go south. Never invest more than you can afford to lose.

NEGLECTING YOUR TIME FRAME

You should never invest without having a time frame in mind. Think about whether or not you are going to need the money that you are pouring into an investment before you enter the trade. You should also decide how long - called the *time horizon* - you will need to save for your retirement, college education, a down payment for your home, or your children.

If you plan to accumulate wealth to purchase a house, it can be thought of as more of a medium-term time frame. But, if you invest with the plan of financing a college tuition, then you could view it as more of a long-term investment. If you are saving for your retirement, which is thirty years from now, then what happens in the market this year or the next should not be one of your major concerns. Once you have a grasp of your horizon, you will be able to track down investments that fit its profile and frame.

NOT MAKING USE OF STOP-LOSS ORDERS

This is one of the biggest signs that you do not have a plan. There are a wide variety of stop orders available, and they are all able to limit losses that are caused by adverse movements in stock, or by the stock market as wholly. These orders are automatically executed once the parameters that you have set have been met.

Tight stops usually entail that your losses will be capped before that can become extreme. But, there is the risk that stop orders on long positions might be carried out at levels below what you have specified, should there be a sudden lowering of the security gap, which happened to several inventors during the Flash Crash.

Even with this thought in mind, the risks of stopping out at a price that was not planned is far outweighed by the benefits that stop orders provide. A corollary to this mistake that traders make is when a trader cancels a stop order on losing a trade right before it can be caused because they think that the trend in price could reverse.

Allowing Your Losses to Accumulate

One of the greatest aspects of successful traders and investors is how they are able to speedily take a small loss if a trade does not go according to plan, and progress to their next trading idea. On the other hand, less successful traders can become immobilized with fear if a trade counters their plans.

They might hold on to a losing position instead of raking fast action to cap the loss, in the hopes that the trade may eventually work out. A losing trade can end up having your trade capital tied up for a long time, and could result in severe depletion of capital and mounting losses.

Averaging Up or Down

Averaging down in a blue-chip stock on a long position might work out for investors with a long-term investment horizon, but it might lead to something rather unfortunate for traders who are trading securities that are more volatile and come with greater risks. Some of the greatest trading failures in the history of the market have taken place because a trader kept adding to a position that was losing, and eventually had to cut the position entirely when the extent of the loss became unreasonable.

Traders also go short frequently, more so than investors who are more conservative, and will usually average up, since the security is advancing instead of retreating. This is just as risky and is another common mistake that many new investors make.

NOT KNOWING WHEN TO ACCEPT YOUR LOSSES

Investors all too often fail to accept the plain fact that they are only human and that they are going to make mistakes - just like the great investors. Whether one of your longtime big earners has suddenly taken a bad turn, or you hastily made a stock purchase, the best thing you should do is accept your losses.

The worst thing to do would be to let your pride cloud your thinking and maintain an investment that is clearly losing. Or, even worse, purchase more of the stock since it is now cheaper. You would be surprised as to how often this mistake is made, and those who do make it do it by comparing the 52-week high of the stock with the current share price. Many folks that use this gauge assume that share prices that share prices that have fallen represent good purchases. But, there was a reason that the drop happened in the first place, and it is up to you to analyze why it happened.

FALLING FOR FALSE BUY SIGNALS

The resignation of a CEO, deteriorating fundamentals, or heightened competition are all plausible causes for stock to lower in price. These very same conditions also provide some great clues to indicate that the stock may not increase soon. A company could be worthless at the moment for fundamental reasons, and it is essential that you always maintain a keen eye, as a low price for shares could also be a false buy signal.

You should never buy stocks in the bargain basement. There is a compelling fundamental reason for a decline in price in most cases. Instead, do your research and analyze the outlook of a stock before you decide to invest. You will want to invest in companies that are going to experience sustained growth in the years to come. The future operating performance of a company has very little to do with the price that you bought its shares.

MAKING A PURCHASE WITH TOO MUCH MARGIN

Margin is using money that you have borrowed from your broker to acquire securities, often options and futures. Even though margins can aid you in more money, they can also increase your losses by just as much, if not more. You should ensure that you have a good understanding of how margin works, and how your broker might require you to sell any positions that you already have.

The worst thing a new investor or trader could do is get carried away with what feels like free money. If you are using margin and your investment does not go as planned, you could have a hefty debt obligation for nothing. Ask yourself if you would buy stocks using your credit card. You wouldn't. Excessively using margin is basically the same thing, usually just at a lower rate of interest.

Additionally, when you use margin, you will have to keep a much keener eye on your positions. Exaggerated losses and gains that come with the small movements in price can cause disaster. If you do not have the knowledge or time to monitor your positions and make decisions about them constantly, and their values drop, your broker will sell your stock to cover any of your losses.

Use margin sparingly as a new trader, if you use it at all, and only use it once you understand the risks that are associated. It can force you to sell all of your positions at the bottom, which is the point that you should be in the market for a big turnaround.

HERD MENTALITY

This is also another very commonly made mistake by new investors. They blindly obey the herd and might end up paying too much for popular stocks or might initiate short positions in securities that have already plummeted and could be on the verge of turning around. Even though more experienced traders follow the mantra that the trend is your friend, it is because they are used to leaving trades when they become overcrowded.

However, new traders might stay in a trade after the smart money has left it. They could also lack the confidence needed to take an approach that is contrary to the trend when it is required of them.

TOO MUCH FINANCIAL TELEVISION

This last one might seem quite silly, but there is pretty much nothing that financial news can offer you that will help you reach your goals. There are hardly any newsletters that could give you anything valuable, and even if there were, how would you be able to identify them in advance?

If someone truly did have trading advice, profitable stock tips, or the secret formula to making it big, would they talk about it on TV or sell it to you for $50 a month? Nope. They would keep it to themselves, make their millions, and then have absolutely no need to sell a newsletter to make their living.

So what's the solution? Stop watching so much financial television and reading newsletters. Spend more time curating your investment plan and sticking to it.

Conclusion

Thanks for making it through to the end of this book. Let's hope it was informative and able to provide you with all of the tools you need to achieve your goals whatever they may be.

The next step is to put some of these strategies into practice and start realizing profits. However, before any wealth generating strategy is implemented, it must be well understood and practiced until proficiency is attained. For instance, money markets are high-risk investments and inexperienced traders stand to lose a lot of money.

Professional traders and investors have a wide variety of investment vehicles to choose from. These range from options trading to trading in stocks, bonds, and currencies. We also have REITs, IPOs, and all the others. A good portfolio is one that is well diversified so that risks are minimized while profits are maximized. Some traders can choose to invest through funds such as mutual funds and electronically traded funds. This way, investors can benefit without having to do all the work themselves.

Finally, if you found this book useful in any way, a review on Amazon is always appreciated!

Personal Notes